ART AND HISTO

RHODES

LINDOS - KAMIROS - IALYSSOS - EMBONAS

Text by
VASSILIA PETSA-TZOUNAKOU

Consultant
MICHAEL ARFARAS

Publication created and designed by Casa Editrice Bonechi
Graphic design and photographic research by Serena de Leonardis
Graphics and layout by Maria Rosanna Malagrinò
Editing by Rita Bianucci
Text and captions by Vassilia Petsa-Tzounakou
Consultant: Michael Arfaras
Translation by Vassilia Petsa-Tzounakou
Drawings by Stefano Benini

Printed in Italy by Centro Stampa Editoriale Bonechi.

Photographs from the Archives of Casa Editrice Bonechi
taken by Paolo Giambone *and* Andrea Pistolesi.
The photograph on page 5 is by Gianni Dagli Orti.

INTRODUCTION

GEOGRAPHY - HISTORY

Rhodes, the largest island in the Greek Dodecanese, is situated in the southeast of the Aegean, opposite the intricately winding south shoreline of Asia Minor. According to myth, the island took its name from Rhode, a sea nymph, daughter of Aphrodite and wife of the Sun God Helios. Home of great athletes in antiquity, Rhodes was praised by Pindar in his 7th Olympionicus, written in 464 B.C. to celebrate the Olympic victories of Diagoras of Rhodes.

Pottery, stone utensils and tools of bone, flint and obsidian prove the existence of widespread human presence in neolithic times. Most of the sites already explored are along or near the wind-protected southeast coast. Minoan and Mycenaean civilization spread from Ialyssos and Kamiros, on the northwest coast.

Myth and archaeological evidence agree as to the arrival of an Achaean tribe from Argolid in the 15th century B.C. A Bronze Age settlement was established at the site of ancient Ialyssos, on Mt. Phileremos. In the next three centuries, pottery of a Rhodian Mycenean type reached other Mediterranean lands due to flourishing commerce. During the Dorian invasion at the end of the 12th century B.C., Heracleides Tlepolemos and his people settled on Ialyssos, Kamiros and Lindos. In 700 B.C., the Doric Hexapolis was founded by the above three Rhodian cities, Cos, Cnidus and Halicarnassus; the Sanctuary of Apollo Triopios in Cnidus was their seat. In the 7th century B.C., Rhodians built colonies in Asia Minor, Magna Grecia, on the Mediterranean coast of contemporary France and on the Valearids. At the same time they dominated the goods trade in the east Mediterranean.

Ancient Rhodes had a strong economy and a naval force. It therefore was a target for military and economic alliance or subjugation. In 491/490 B.C., Darius I of Persia dispatched strong military and naval forces which, nevertheless, failed to subjugate the island. In 480 B.C. however, Rhodians reinforced the Persian fleet in the sea battle at Salamis. They subsequently joined the First Athenian Confederacy in 478/477 B.C., after the defeat of the Persians. Aiming to best serve the interests of his homeland, Rhodian leader Dorieus withdrew from the Athenian Confederacy during the Peloponnesian War. He sided with the Spartans and supported their fleet against the Athenians in the sea-battle at Symi, in 412/411 B.C.

The island's fame was to be further promoted, when settlers from Ialyssos, Kamiros and Lindos jointly founded the city of Rhodes in 408 B.C., on an orthogonal grid plan, in the Hippodameian manner.

The Rhodians established friendly relations with Alexander the Great when it had become clear that the Macedonians had won supremacy over the Persians. They also forged good trade connections in Alexandria, Egypt. When one of Alexander's successors demanded that the Rhodians turn against Egypt, he received a refusal. As a consequence, Demetrios Poliorketes attacked Rhodes. His year-long siege ended with a settlement.

During the era of the Roman expansion in the Mediterranean, Rhodes was both a considerable ally and an opponent of the Romans. The Rhodian admiral Eudamos defeated Hannibal, the formidable enemy of the Romans, at the sea-battle in Side, Pamphylia, in 190 B.C.. However, Rhodian sovereignty in Caria and Lycia on the coast of Asia Minor was lost to the Romans in 167 B.C.. An agreement was reached between the Rhodians and the Romans in 164 B.C., making an obligation for mutual alliance. At the same time, prominent Romans began to arrive in Rhodes to receive instruction by philosophers and orators. Rhodians supported Roman ranks during the Third Carthaginian War (167 B.C.) and in the Mithridatic Wars (88-63 B.C.). As the island supported Julius Caesar in the Civil War, it was subsequently besieged, captured and plundered by Cassius in 42 B.C. In the years that followed, Rhodes lost its naval power and its destiny was determined by the will of the Roman emperors. After the fierce raids by the Goths, a Germanic tribe, in A.D. 263-269, Diocletian united Rhodes with the Roman Province of the Islands and made it its capital at the end of the third century A.D.

Little is known about the history of Rhodes in the Early Christian years. The island was temporarily seized from the Byzantines by the Persian King Chosroes II, in A.D. 620. The parts of the bronze Colossus of Rhodes, which had lain on the ground since the destructive earthquakes of 225 B.C., were sold by Arabs under the Chaliph Muawiyah in 653 B.C. The Byzantine fleet launched attacks against the Saracen pirates from Rhodes in A.D. 718. A fleet led by Harun Al Rashid, Chaliph of the Baghdad Abbasids, raided Rhodes in A.D. 807. During the Third Crusade, Richard the Lionheart of England and Philip II of France came to Rhodes and recruited mercenaries. Byzantine nobleman, Leo Gavalas, ruled Rhodes from 1204-1240. After his death, the island was officially under Byzantine command; however, in reality, it was under the control of Genoese admirals.

Knight rule commenced in 1309. From that time, the island became the bone of contention in a struggle for religious supremacy in the Mediterranean. Finally, in 1522, cunning Suleiman the Magnificent, the Ottoman ruler, subjugated Rhodes.

In 1911, Italy declared war against Turkey and Italian forces captured Rhodes in May 1912. The Italian occupation lasted 33 years, until the end of World War II. In May 1945, the Italian Commander of Rhodes was handed over by the Germans to the Allied Forces, who collaborated with the Greek Sacred Regiment to liberate the island. Power was transferred to the Greek admiral Pericles Ioannides by the Provisional British Command on 31 May 1947. The formal union of the Dodecanese with Greece was declared in Rhodes almost a year later.

Page 2: Bronze deer on a pedestal. Entrance to the Mandraki Harbor.

Imaginary drawing of the Colossus of Rhodes according to oral tradition.

ANCIENT RHODIAN LETTERS

From archaic times, Rhodes rose as an independent hub of Hellenic intellectualism. It gradually became a pole of attraction for intellectuals from other lands. Leading savants, like Athenian rhetorician Aeschines, settled on the island. Rhodians who had studied abroad returned to Rhodes, like peripatetic philosopher Eudemus, who had been a student of Aristoteles.
Apollonius Rhodius, third century B.C. poet and philosopher, was actually born in Alexandria or Naucratis in Egypt. In Rhodes, he revised his much acclaimed epic poem Argonautica and produced so much intellectual work that he was given the cognomen Rhodius.
Intellectual activity in Rhodes manifested itself in a multitude of disciplines: philosophy, oratory, historiography, poetry and epigram, medicine, geography, astronomy and mathematics. Many savants occupied themselves with more than one discipline. Important astronomic observations and some of the first geographic measurements were made in Rhodes.

SAMPLES OF ANCIENT RHODIAN ART

Monumental works of painting and sculpture were exhibited in public places. They bore witness to the flourishing civilization and the sturdy economy of the island. Paintings by classical painter Parrhasius of Ephesus were on display in Rhodes and in Lindos. Works by Apelles, the official painter of the Macedonian court, were to be found in Rhodes, just as was a colossal four-horse bronze chariot by Lyssipus, Alexander's favorite portrait sculptor.
The Colossus of Rhodes (ca. 300 B.C.), bronze statue of the Sun God Helios measuring 31 meters, was made by sculptor Chares of Lindos. It was considered one of the Seven Wonders of the Ancient World. According to oral tradition, it stood astride the harbor entrance and ships passed underneath.
The Winged Victory of Samothrace, now in the Louvre, and the bronze Sleeping Cupid in the Metropolitan Museum of Art in New York, are attributed to Rhodian Hellenistic workshops. The statue of the Victory was probably a Rhodian offering to the Sanctuary of the Great Gods in Samothrace.
A monumental Rhodian sculpture group of the Roman era showed the sons of Antiope punishing Dirce by tying her onto the horns of a raging bull. It is known in ancient literature and from a Roman copy, Taurus Farnese, in the National Museum of Naples, Italy.

The walled city and its environs, and the ports of the City of Rhodes. Illustration from a 16th century book of sailing directions in the Old Library of St. Mark's, Venice.

s: nicol

RHODES
THE CITY OF THE KNIGHTS

Left page: South entrance. Palace of the Grand Master.

The Palace of the Grand Master and part of the city fortifications. Northeast seaward view.

HISTORY OF THE CITY OF THE KNIGHTS

A great part of the island of Rhodes was ceded against payment to the Knights of the Order of St. John of Jerusalem by Genoese admiral Vignolo da Vignoli in 1306. By 1309, the Knights had gradually conquered the entire island. In the 213 years of their stay in Rhodes, they undertook considerable building work; in the Old Town of Rhodes, which is still called City of the Knights, they left indelible samples of their architecture. The city walls and the buildings of the Knights were restored by the Italians in the early 20th century and they are now preserved by the Greek State.

The medieval town was surrounded by an external wall and a moat. It was divided into two unequal, almost rectangular parts by an internal wall. Greeks, western laymen and Jews inhabited Chora, the largest part of the Old Town, in the south. The Knights lived in the smallest of the two parts, known as Castello or Collachium, to the north. In this part were the Palace of the Grand Master, the Inns and the Hospital of the Knights. The members of the Order were divided into Tongues, according to their place of origin. Each Tongue was housed in its own building or Inn, where officials and guests of the Order lived and where the Knights dined.

Western thought and the centuries-long local Byzantine tradition mingled in the cultural life of Rhodes during the era of the Knights. Greek and

Western scholars and artists gathered in the court of the Grand Masters. In the second half of the 15th century, the Greeks regained the right to have their own Orthodox Metropolitan under the Pope, and they renovated or built new churches and monasteries. Life in Rhodes at the end of the 15th century was described by the Greek poet of that time Emmanuel Georgillas Limenites.
The main concern of the Knights was the repulsion of Islam. An Egyptian fleet besieged Rhodes in 1440 and 1444 but it was turned back both times. The Ottoman Turks set up two major sieges forcing the Knights to bolster their fortifications and to spend a good part of their financial resources. Grand Master Pierre d'Aubusson warded off the danger in 1480. In a diplomatic move, in 1482 he granted asylum to Prince Djem, who lay claim to the Turkish throne. In remembrance of the victory in 1480, the erection of Our Lady of the Victory was started in Gothic style in the southeast corner of Chora; the church was never completed. In 1522, following a siege and treaty, Rhodes was handed over to the Ottomans. The Knights and 4,000 Rhodians left for Crete. Marking a new era in the town's history, Suleiman the Magnificent prayed for the first time in the Byzantine church of Haghia Aikaterini, which was converted into a mosque called Ilk Mihrab or First Prayer Niche.

Left page. Top: The remains of Naillac Tower and the cylindrical Trébuc Tower.
Bottom: The Palace of the Grand Master.

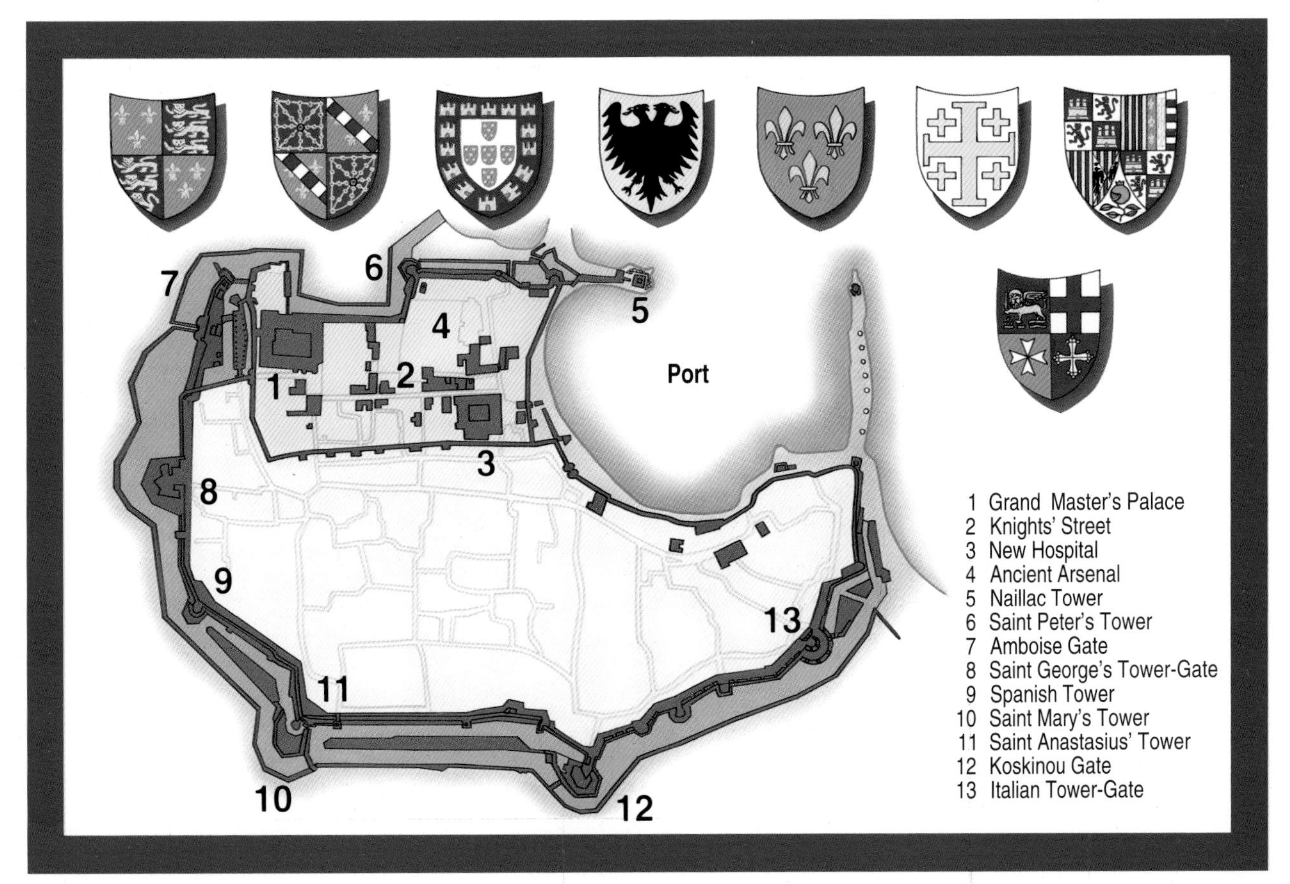

Plan of the City of the Knights. From left to right, the coats of arms of England, Navarre, Portugal, Germany, France-Auvergne, Provence and Castille-Aragon; below, the coat of arms of the Maritime Republics.

Left page: The moat, the advance wall and a rectangular defensive tower on the curtain wall.

The Gate of Liberty (1924) links the Old with the New Town.

A VISIT TO THE CITY OF THE KNIGHTS

Plateia Symis is accessible from the Gate of Liberty on the north walls, and from Arsenal Gate. The Municipal Gallery is housed in a 15th century reconstructed building in the square and contains fine samples of 20th century Greek painting and works by folk painter Theophilos. In adjacent Argyrokastrou Square, the Inn of the Tongue of Auvergne (1507) has three arches on the ground floor facade and an upstairs loggia. In the same square, the Old Hospital of the Knights had also been used as an armory; it now houses the Greek Archaeological Service. Like other buildings dating from the first building phase of the Knights, it has a plain facade. The main entrance was later constructed in the interior of the apse of the Hospital's Gothic chapel.

Our Lady of the Castle (11th century) is situated opposite the entrance to the Street of the Knights. Its choir apse lies next to the walls and culminates in a tower without defensive function; the tower merely contributed to the visual adaptation of the building to the architecture of the walls. Initially the seat of the Orthodox Metropolitan, the church had an inscribed-cross plan with a dome. In the first building phase of the Knights, it became the seat of the Catholic Archbishop. The interior of the church was remodelled into three aisles and a transept. Gothic ribbed groin-vaults were added to the ceiling, pointed arches and stained glass to the windows. During

the Turkish occupation, the church was converted into a mosque called Enderoum or Kandouri. It now houses a collection of Byzantine art.
The Inn of the Tongue of England (1483) on Museum Square was destroyed and later rebuilt by the Italians in 1919, on the basis of drawings by Belgian traveller Rottiers, who visited Rhodes in the early 19th century.

Top: Arnaldo Gate, inner passage. In the distance is the entrance to the Hospital of the Knights. Bottom: The Marine Gate. The relief figures of the Virgin Mary, St. John and St. Peter are set in a framed Gothic niche between the massive horseshoe-shaped towers. The coats of arms are of the Order, of France and of Grand Master Pierre d'Aubusson.

Left page. Top: Fishing boats at the Commercial Harbor. Bottom: The road from the Commercial Harbor to Mandraki and Arsenal Gate, on the left.

Argyrokastrou Square. The Old Hospital of the Knights and an Early Christian baptistery incorporated in a fountain in the middle of the square.

Right page. Our Lady of the Castle. Top and bottom left: The west facade from the north and south respectively. To the north of the church is a renovated arched building. The orthogonal frame over the main entrance contained a fresco probably dating from a little after 1480, which perhaps depicted Saints and Knights hierachically arranged, with the Virgin Mary at the top. Bottom right: The transept arches on both sides and the ribbed groin-vaults over the nave and choir.

The Street of the Knights. View of the north side.

Right page. Top and bottom right: The Inn of the Tongue of France. First floor detail and view of the facade respectively. The ornamental mouldings and window frames, the gargoyles, the semicylindrical turrets and the false crenellations add distinctive grace to the facade. Together in the square frame are the coats of arms of France and of Pierre d'Aubusson. Below is the coat of arms of Philippe de l'Isle Adam. Bottom left: The Inn of the Tongue of Italy. Detail of the facade with the coat of arms of Fabrizio del Carretto framed by an ogive pointed arch.

THE STREET OF THE KNIGHTS

One of the most beautiful medieval streets, the cobbled Street of the Knights, starts from the Church of Our Lady of the Castle, at the edge of Museum Square, and culminates in the entrance square of the Palace of the Grand Master. Most of the structures in this street belong to the second building phase, after the Turkish siege of the town in 1480. They are made of well-hewn, isodomically arranged local sandstone. They are distinguished by their fine Gothic decoration of sculpted door and window frames and of horizontal mouldings, which make a pleasant contrast to the otherwise plain surface of the wall. The Inns of the Knights were two-storeyed and bore on the facades the coats of arms of the Order and of the officials who had played an important role in their erection, extension or repair. Behind the Renaissance-like arcades of the ground floor, there were storage rooms and an interior courtyard. The main entrance was on one side of the facade and stairs led to the rooms on the first floor.

Top left: The Chapel of France. Detail of the facade with a statue of the Madonna and Child in a Gothic canopied niche. Top right: The north side of the street showing the same Chapel and, next to it, the House of the Prior of France. The arched passageway nearest to the picture plane belongs to the Inn of Spain on the south side of the street and joins it to the Inn of Provence. Bottom: The arch at the top of the Street of the Knights.

Left page: The Inn of the Tongue of Provence. Main entrance. The coats of arms are of the Order, of France, of Fabrizio del Carretto and of the Prior of Toulouse F. Flotta.

The Palace of the Grand Master. South view.

Next page. The inner courtyard. Top: View from the east. Bottom: The north loggia and the niches with the statues of the Roman emperors.

THE PALACE OF THE GRAND MASTER

The Palace of the Grand Master is situated in the northwest corner of the walls, in the highest part of the Collachium. It was the fortified residence of the highest official and the administrative center of the Order. Its construction started soon after the arrival of the Knights in Rhodes, on the remains of the 7th century Byzantine Acropolis. It suffered great damage in 1856, during the Turkish rule, with the explosion of ammunition stored in the church of the patron saint of the Order, St. John of the Collachium, south of the palace. When the Italian Cesare Maria de Vecchi was Commander of the Dodecanese, a radical reconstruction took place in 1937-40, so that the building could be used as a summer residence by the Italian high officials of that time. The role of the Palace as a decision-making center was renewed in December 1988, when its rooms were used during the European Summit Meeting.

The Palace is built around the perimeter of an inner courtyard measuring 50x40 meters. Situated in its south side, the main entrance is flanked by two horseshoe-shaped tall towers, reminiscent of those of the Marine Gate, which is the town's impressive entrance point from the sea. In the center of the inner coutyard, there are wells and, in niches along its north side, statues of Roman emperors from the early 20th century Italian excavations at the Odeum in Cos. Shady stoas border the south and the east

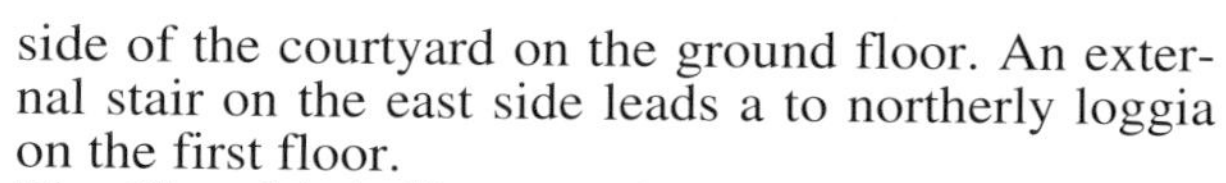

side of the courtyard on the ground floor. An external stair on the east side leads a to northerly loggia on the first floor.
The Chapel is halfway up the stair from the covered entrance passageway to the first floor of the Palace. It contains a bronze copy of Donatello's St. Nicholas and marble relief depictions of scenes from the life of Christ and the Saints by early 20th century Italian sculptor Montoleone.
The rooms of the Palace were decorated with mosaics and statues from Cos and with functional and decorative objects of Western European and Oriental art of the 16th-19th centuries. A copy of the Laocoon group is also on display at the Palace. The first century B.C. original by Rhodian sculptors Agesander, Athenodorus and Polydorus is now in the Vatican Museum.

Top and next page, bottom: Views of the hypostyle hall with the Hellenistic trophy and Late Roman and Early Christian mosaic floors from the island of Cos. Reused granite columns with Early Christian capitals support the freely reconstructed row of arches. During the era of the Grand Masters, the Palace was decorated with carved wooden furniture, carpets, tapestries and precious vases. Bottom: The broad, vaulted, marble staircase leading to the first floor of the Palace.

Next page. Top: Within a square frame, an apotropaic head of the Gorgon Medusa with motifs radiating out from the center of the composition. Mosaic of the Late Hellenistic era. The art of the mosaic spread to Cos and Rhodes from the 3rd century B.C. depicting themes from mythology, geometric and naturalistic compositions.

Top: View of a room with ribbed groin-vaults and Renaissance wooden pews. The windows of the Palace afford magnificent views of the city and the sea. Bottom: Copy of the Laocoon group. Like the Taurus Farnese, another sculptural group of the Roman era, the Laocoon depicts a favorite theme of that time, namely human agony in combat with uncontrolled natural forces.

Next page. Mosaics from Cos made with quadrangular pieces of stone. Top: Sea Horse and Numph, 1st century B.C. Bottom: Gladiator and Tiger, Hellenistic period.

Left page. Another room in the Palace with a ceiling of timber and a freely reconstructed row of arches. On the floor is a 5th century A.D. mosaic with an elaborate geometric composition from the Early Christian basilica of Haghios Johannes in Cos. In the wall niches are 17th century wooden candleholders in the shape of angels. The masonry of the reception rooms of the Palace is plain, with isodomically arranged local sandstone. Wall paintings adorn rooms on the ground floor, on the mezzanine and in the residential quarters.

Top: Room of the mosaic with the Nine Muses. Over the fireplace is the grandiose coat of arms of the Italian dynasty.
Bottom: Late Hellenistic mosaic depicting the heads of the Nine Muses and their attributes, set in medallions.

The Hospital of the Knights. Bottom: View of the inner courtyard of the Hospital showing the two-storeyed, arched facade.

Next page. Top: Late Hellenistic lion holding a bull's head in its front paws. Made of local grey marble. Bottom: View of the inner courtyard of the Hospital.

THE ARCHAEOLOGICAL MUSEUM OF RHODES

The Archaeological Museum of Rhodes is housed in the Hospital of the Knights. Its construction started in 1440 but it was completed during the second building phase of the Knights.

The seven ground floor arches on Museum Square led to storage rooms. The Chapel of the Hospital was on the first floor over the main entrance with the Gothic portal. Architecturally, the Hospital reflects the eastern tradition of buildings such as Byzantine hospices and oriental caravanserais, which developed around a central courtyard in one or two arched storeys.

Some of the Museum's exhibits are presented in the next pages. Separate mention must be made of the silver coins of the ancient city of Rhodes. On one face, they bore the head of the Sun God Helios. On the other was a rose in relief with an inscription of the coin's origin.

Top: The funerary stele of Kalliarista from a cemetery in the city of Rhodes, dedicated by the deceased woman's husband, Damocles. First half of 4th century B.C. Bottom left: The funerary stele of Krito and Timarista from a cemetery in Kamiros, showing a tender last farewell. End of 5th century B.C. Bottom right: The Aphrodite of Rhodes (1st century B.C.).

Left page. Top: View of the archaic sculpture room. Head and torsoes of Kouroi (550-520 B.C.), found in Kamiros. Bottom left: Marble head of the Sun God Helios (2nd century B.C.). Bottom right: Fragment of a female funerary statue. Second half of 4th century B.C.

Top: View of a room in the Museum with a Late Hellenistic statue of Aphrodite of the Arles type. Bottom: Three-sided Archaistic Late Hellenistic sculpture found on the Acropolis of Rhodes. It contains three sculpted images of the Goddess Hecate of the Underworld. The goddess wears an archaic chiton in the manner of the Athenian Korae and bears a cylindrical headdress and a three-legged caldron on her head.

Next page. View of the Museum garden with Hellenistic and Roman exhibits.
Bottom left: Dolphins from a funerary monument, made of grey marble. Middle of 2nd century B.C.
Bottom right: Mosaic floor from the Early Christian basilica of Arkasa in Karpathos (6th century A.D.), now in the sunken courtyard of the Museum garden.

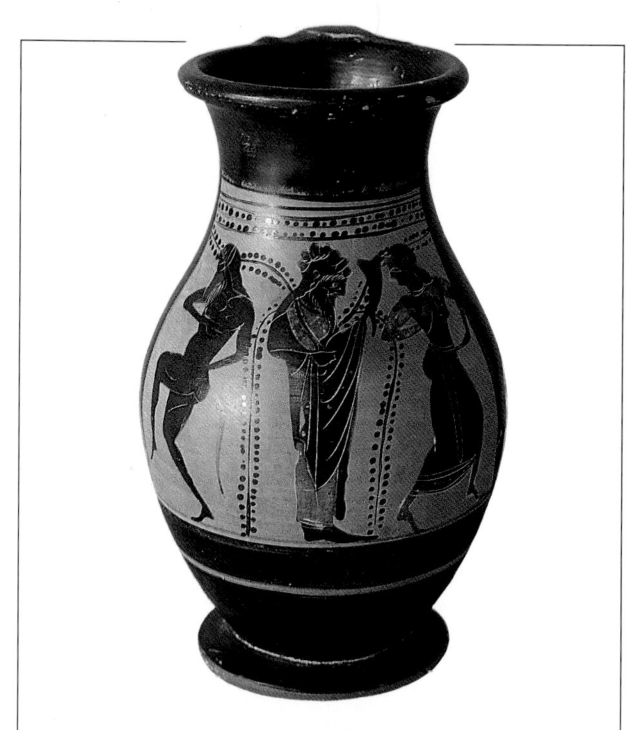

Top left: Archaic clay idol connected with the cult of Demeter and Persephone. Top right: Attic olpae, or wine vessel, with Dionysian themes.
Bottom: Black-figured amphora (6th century B.C.) with banded decoration. Human figures, wild animals and mythological monsters are depicted in formal compositions.

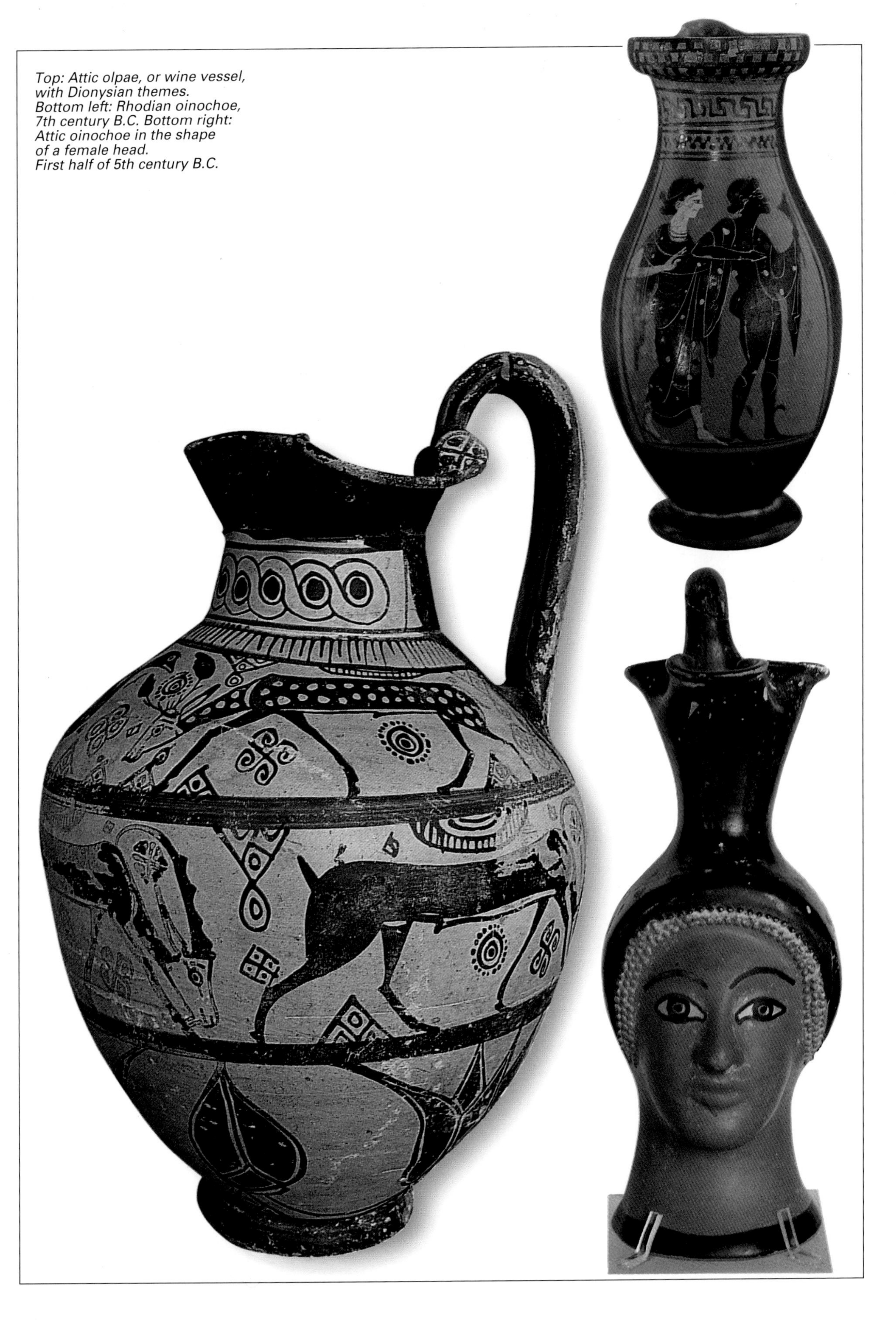

Top: Attic olpae, or wine vessel, with Dionysian themes. Bottom left: Rhodian oinochoe, 7th century B.C. Bottom right: Attic oinochoe in the shape of a female head. First half of 5th century B.C.

The infirmary ward of the Hospital of the Knights. It now contains coats of arms and funerary reliefs from the era of the Knights. The Chapel was in the apse with a flamboyant Gothic arch, on the longer side of the room, over the Hospital's main entrance. The coats of arms of the Order and of Grand Master Pierre d'Aubusson can be seen at the point where the arches meet the columns.

Right page: Archaic clay female head. First half of 5th century B.C.

Views of the Museum interior. On the left, a Dodecanesian 'pataros', which is an elevated sleeping area sheltered by a screen carved in wood.

THE MUSEUM OF POPULAR ART

The Museum of Popular Art is in Argyrokastrou Square. One of its highlights is the Rhodian sperveri, a silk-embroidered curtain which adorned the nuptial bed. The Museum also contains a great variety of ceramic plates which were originally made in Asia Minor; they are known as Rhodian or Lindian plates because their production spread on the island, too. They date from the 16th-18th centuries and depict boats and a variety of motifs from the plant and animal world. Local costumes, multicolored embroidery, painted wooden chests, wood carved furniture, decorative objects and items of everyday use provide a colorful picture of art and tradition in the Dodecanese.

Ippokratous Square. View of the southeast side.

THE CITY WITHIN THE WALLS

Churches, public buildings, shops and houses were to be found within the city walls in the era of the Knights. During the Turkish rule, which lasted approximately four centuries, the Greeks were obliged to leave Chora and to settle in areas outside the walls. The churches were converted into sites of Muslim worship and six new mosques were constructed in central locations.

There are 24 well-known Byzantine churches in the Old Town. They date from the Christian era in the history of the city which lasted about 13 centuries, including the rule of the Knights. They can be classified into five architectural types. Fifteenth century Haghios Georghios, with its elegant elevated dome, is the only one with a quatrefoil plan. As an architectural type, it derives its plan from concentric buildings such as the Roman mausolea and the Early Christian martyria. A Franciscan monastery was housed in Haghios Georghios during the rule of the Knights. During the Turkish occupation, a Muslim theological seminary was founded there. It is known as Chourmali Medrese, or the School at the Date Palm. Haghios Georghios is located near the Bastion of St. George, on the west side of the walls.

Three fresco-painting styles can be distinguished in the Byzantine churches on the island of Rhodes: the Byzantine, the West European and the eclectic, or mixed style. In the Old Town, thirteenth century

Castellania (1507). An Aegean-type external staircase leads to the first floor balcony. A marble relief lintel in Renaissance style can be seen on the left.
The ground floor arcade and the horizontal arrangement of the facade are also Renaissance traits. The coat of arms of Grand Master Emery d'Amboise is set in a flamboyant Gothic frame.

Next page. Top: View of the Marine Gate from Ippokratous Square. Bottom: Our Lady of the Burgum (ca. 1400). Pointed choir apses.

Haghios Phanourios on Dorieus Square has a free-cross plan with a dome and contains well preserved 13th-15th century frescoes in the Byzantine style. A fresco dating from 1335-1336 depicts the donors and two children. In the southwest part of the Old Town, Haghia Aikaterini, or Ilk Mihrab, is a three-aisled, vaulted church with an irregular plan made up of three trapezoids due to the location where it was erected. It contains 14th-15th century frescoes also executed in the Byzantine style. On the inner face of the western wall, over the entrance, is a fresco depicting Christ and the donors.
In the southwest part of the Old Town, Haghios Nikolaos has gothic architectural elements and frescoes of mixed Byzantine and West European style, dating from the era of the Knights. Haghia Triada, or Dolapli Mesjid (14th-15th century), a Byzantine church with a free-cross plan and a dome, is situated in the southeast part of the Old Town and also contains mixed West European and Byzantine style frescoes. A baptistery or narthex added to the north arm of the cross had a pointed octagonal dome over squinches of an Islamic type.
A remarkable sample of dominant Western influence is a fragment of a fresco in Our Lady of the Castle, depicting Santa Lucia in the Tuscan 14th century manner.
Saint John of the Collachium, Our Lady of the Burgum and Our Lady of the Victory had a Gothic character from the start.
The Muslim Library was founded in 1794 by the Rhodian Muslim Ahmed Chaphouz Aga. It was ini-

RESTAURANT PLAKA SEA FOOD
sea food
ΠΛΑΚΑ
"PLAKA"
RESTAURANT
ROOF GARDEN

Style

tially housed in the Mosque of Murad Reis, outside the city walls. It is now in a building opposite the Mosque of Suleiman and contains Turkish, Arabian and Persian manuscripts, some of which are illuminated, and an anonymous chronicle of the siege in 1522.

The Synagogue was founded in the center of the Jewish quarters in the 16th or 17th century although the Jewish community in Rhodes is considerably older. In the same area, the Hospice of St. Cather-

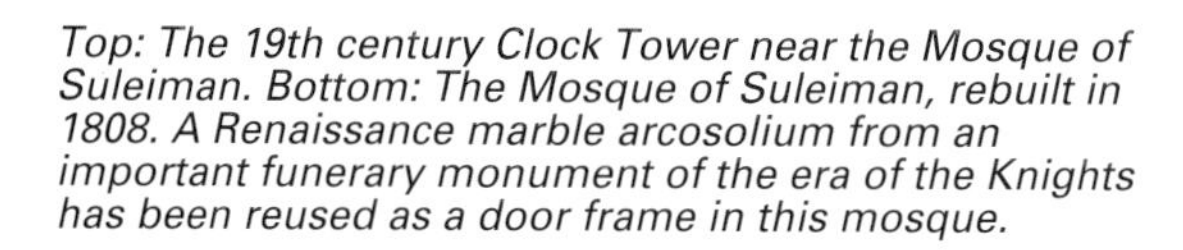

Top: The 19th century Clock Tower near the Mosque of Suleiman. Bottom: The Mosque of Suleiman, rebuilt in 1808. A Renaissance marble arcosolium from an important funerary monument of the era of the Knights has been reused as a door frame in this mosque.

Left page: Top left: The House of the Greek Orthodox Metropolitan on the Square of the Jewish Martyrs is identified by Latin and Greek inscriptions on the building. It dates from the second building phase of the Knights and is characterized by Renaissance symmetry and horizontal aspect. The fountain with the sea horses was constructed by the Italians in the early 20th century. Top right: The Mosque of Suleiman from the east. Bottom: Views of Sokratous Street.

ine, founded by Fra Domenico d'Alemagna, was renovated in 1516 by Costanzo Operti. It provided shelter to Italian Knights on pilgrimage to the Holy Land. On the facade are the coats of arms of Operti and of Grand Master Fabrizio del Carretto. There is also a relief of the wheel, the symbol of St. Catherine's martyrdom.

The building of Castellania, the commercial court of the Knights, bears witness to the flourishing economy in Rhodes during that era. Only the southwest part of the building is preserved. It now houses the Public Library of Rhodes and the Historical Archives of the Dodecanese.

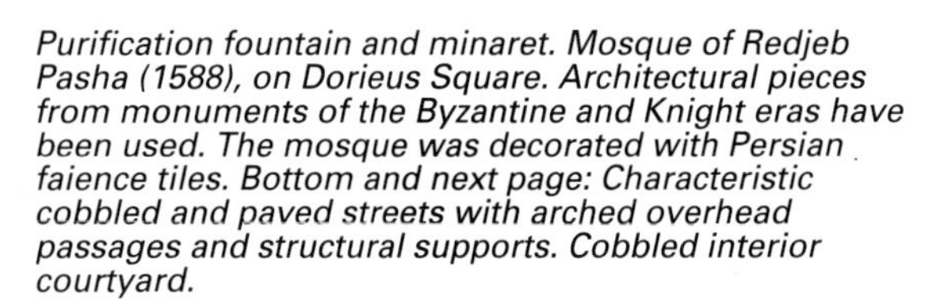

Purification fountain and minaret. Mosque of Redjeb Pasha (1588), on Dorieus Square. Architectural pieces from monuments of the Byzantine and Knight eras have been used. The mosque was decorated with Persian faience tiles. Bottom and next page: Characteristic cobbled and paved streets with arched overhead passages and structural supports. Cobbled interior courtyard.

Bar

Top and bottom: Ippokratous Square, night views. In the picture at the top, the dome of Chandrevan Mosque is outlined in the horizon.

Left page: Top: Recent preservation scaffolding at the Mosque of Sultan Mustafa (1765), on cool Arionos Square. In the architecture of the Mosque, elements from the Christian art of building are combined with the Muslim tradition. The Baths of Mustafa on the same Square are contemporary with the Mosque. Bottom: The Mosque of Ibrahim Pasha (1531), south of Ippokratous Square, is the oldest Islamic sacred edifice in Chora.

THE OLD TOWN AND THE WALLS

At first the Knights found it sufficient to reinforce and repair the 7th and 12th century Byzantine fortifications. From the end of the 14th century, the walls took a new shape. The medieval fortification of the city of Rhodes was based on construction methods brought over by the Knights from their native lands. These methods were influenced by the invention and use of artillery weapons, which was the latest development in the art of warfare. The numerous coats of arms on the walls bear witness to the contribution of the Pope and successive Grand Masters to the repair, maintenance and reinforcement of the walls and the moat.

During the second Turkish siege, each Tongue had undertaken the defense of a particular sector of the walls. The Tongue of Germany had taken over the sector from the Gate d'Amboise, to the west of the Palace, until the Bastion of St. George, along the west line of the walls. In a counterclockwise movement, the Tongue of Auvergne covered a continuous part of the walls until the Tower of Spain. The sector of the Tongue of Spain-Aragon followed, until the Bastion of Our Lady and, along the south side of the walls, the sector of England, until the Bastion of St. John, at Koskinou Gate. The Tongue of Provence had taken over the defense until the Bastion of del Carretto and the Tongue of Italy, the east side, until St. Catherine's gate at the port. The seaward line of the walls was controlled by the Tongue of Castille, while the north sector was occupied by the Tongue of France. The port entrances were guarded by the Fort of France and the Naillac Tower at the entrance to the present day Commercial Harbor, and by the Fort of St. Nicholas, to the north of the medieval town, at the Mandraki harbor entrance. When the Gate d'Amboise (1512) was constructed

The Temple of Aphrodite on Symis Square. Third century B.C., with Roman additions.

Next page. Top: The Gate of Liberty and part of the moat. Bottom: Rectangular defense tower along the west line of the walls.

Top: The Gate of Koskinou. Bottom: The Gate of St. Athanassios.

Left page. Top: The Gate d'Amboise. Bottom: Western view of the Palace and the fortifications

on the northwest corner of the walls, it enclosed three older and smaller ones and created an additional fortified enclosure to the west of the Palace. The two low cylindrical towers flanking the Gate had openings at the top for the positioning of artillery weapons. The square tower at the Bastion of St. George was constructed during the third decade of the 15th century. On the western face, it bears a relief depicting St. George killing the dragon, and the coats of arms of Pope Martin V, of the Order and of Grand Master Antoni de Fluviañ. Defense works were completed under the rule of Grand Masters Pierre d'Aubusson and Villiers de l'Isle Adam, when the Islamic threat had reached a climax. At the

Bastion of St. John, there is a unique marble slab embedded in the wall with a bilingual inscription, in Greek and Italian, dated August 20, 1457. It commemorates the contribution of Greek master mason Manuel Koundes to the fortification works, under the rule of Grand Master Jacques de Milly.
In addition to the Temple of Aphrodite, within the city walls, to the north, was the Sanctuary of Dionysus, which contained important works of art. The Sanctuary of the Sun God Helios must have been at the site of the Palace of the Grand Master; according to recent archaeological research, the Colossus of Rhodes also stood there in antiquity.

The Gate of St. Paul. Top: Cylindrical defense tower. Bottom: The Gate from the west.

Right page: Views of the defense enclosure.

Mandraki. Top: A natural-sponge vendor's stall.
Bottom: Flag masts at the Mole of St. Nicholas.

Next page. Top: Reconstructed medieval mills at Mandraki.
Bottom: The Fort of St. Nicholas (1464-1467).

THE NEW TOWN NEAR THE PORT

The medieval town is surrounded by new quarters to the north, west, and south. During the Italian occupation (1912-1945), some public buildings were constructed to the west of the Mandraki Harbor, on the site of one of the five ports of ancient Rhodes. On the whole, they display a variety of form and style. Although they do not reflect the Aegean style of architecture, they are interesting from a historical point of view. The building of the Prefecture, the former Italian Governor's Palace, is a mixture of

Marine views at Mandraki. Top: View of the Metropolis of Rhodes with the tall bell tower. In the background are the Shipping Companies' Offices and the Port Authority. Bottom: Tourist vessels anchored at the Mole of St. Nicholas.

Next page. Top: The north and the east side of the Palace of the Grand Master. Behind the anchored vessels is part of the Municipal Garden. Bottom: The New Market with elements of Islamic construction and style. On the facade of the tall entrance gate are coats of arms bearing a cross, which was the characteristic symbol of the Order and, by extension, of the Italian state of occupation and, today, of the city of Rhodes.

Venetian Gothic style with elements of Moorish tradition. The Town Hall, the Law Courts, the Port Authority Building, the Post Office, the National Theater and the Hotel des Roses are built in the austere and imposing style of Italian official architecture of the early 20th century. The New Market is a low polygonal structure around an inner courtyard, in the manner of oriental markets. The Church of the Annunciation, which is now the Metropolis of Rhodes, contains frescoes of Byzantine inspiration

NERAIDA
SUN SUN

by the 20th century Greek painter Photis Kondoglou. It was built during the second decade of the Italian occupation as a copy of St. John of the Collachium, on the basis of drawings by the Belgian Rottiers. The Mosque of Murad Reis was built on the site of the Knight's church of St. Antony and of the cemetery of the common Knights, opposite the National Theater and the Prefecture. The Mosque was dedicated to Suleiman the Magnificent's admiral during the last siege of Rhodes. In the Turkish cemetery next to the Mosque, some prominent Muslims lie buried, such as a Shah of Persia, a Prince of Crimea, and the 18th century poet Mohamed Ahmed Efendi. In the same cemetery is the circular mausoleum of Murad Reis.

Top: A beach near the walls. Bottom: Sailboats anchored near the Fort of St. Nicholas.

Left page. Top: The Metropolis of Rhodes.
Bottom: The Prefecture.

Next pages: Dusk at Mandraki.

Top: A view of the Stadium and the Odeum of Ancient Rhodes. Left: Thick vegetation on the hill to the east of the Sanctuary of Athena Polias and Zeus Polieus.

Next Page: The Sanctuary of Apollo Pythios.

THE ACROPOLIS OF RHODES

The ancient Acropolis of Rhodes was at Haghios Stephanos, an elevation to the northwest of the Old Town. The texts of treaties with other states were kept in the Sanctuary of Athena Polias and Zeus Polieus, the protectors of the town. On the green slope of the hill, to the east of the Sanctuary, were caves devoted to the Nymphs and stoas that were part of the aqueduct. The Sanctuary of Apollo Pythios was next to the Stadium and the Odeum.
Reconstruction work was carried out by Italian archaeologists in the early 20th century. The Acropolis was an important center for religion and for intellectual, artistic and athletic activity. The Gymnasium of the ancient city also lay in the vicinity.

STRINTZIS LINES

THE NORTHWEST COAST

The northwest coast offers tourist, archaeological and historic sights. Ialyssos and Kamiros, the two important archaic city-states along the coast, controlled the territory that surrounded them. Archaeological finds from ancient Ialyssia and Kamiris are exhibited in the Archaeological Museum in the Old Town of Rhodes.
The Byzantine fortresses of Phileremos, Cretenia and Monolithos were built at strategic locations. During the rule of the Knights, they were improved and they played a significant role in the defense of the island.
Mount Phileremos is found south of the tourist Bay of Ialyssos, near the city of Rhodes. Near the picturesque Bay of Glyphada is Mount Atabyros (1,215 m.), the highest mountain in Rhodes, barren of trees. Its neighboring Mount Akramitis is covered by lush vegetation, like Mount Prophet Elias, which is a popular recreation area. In the southernmost part of the northwest coast is the Bay of Apolakkia, where one can enjoy a quiet vacation near the sea and visit scattered remains of ancient, Early Christian, Byzantine and medieval monuments.
The climate is healthy, as in the rest of the island. Sunshine and northerly winds prevail, while rainfall is the highest in the Dodecanese. The local economy is largely based on the tourist industry, with less emphasis on commerce, folk arts, and on the cultivation of slopes and valleys.

Left page: Beaches near the City of Rhodes.

Lush vegetation reaches the sandy beaches of Rhodes.

PHILEREMOS

In the east part of the plateau on top of green Mount Phileremos, the remains of a three-aisled Early Christian basilica dedicated to the Virgin Mary (5th-6th century A.D.) are superimposed on the ruins of the Temple of Athena Polias. On the north aisle of the basilica, an aisleless church was built either in Byzantine times or during the era of the Knights. Two Gothic chapels were erected in the northeast corner of the basilica at the end of the 15th century. They belong to the Knights' Monastery of Our Lady, which was rebuilt during the Italian occupation. Painted in an eclectic mixture of Western and Byzantine style, the icon of the Monastery is now in Saint Petersburg.
Toward the center of the plateau, in the east part, are the ruins of a 10th century Byzantine monastery and

Top: The entrance staircase to the Monastery. Bottom: The bell tower of the reconstructed Monastery. Surrounded by a protective rail is the baptistery of an Early Christian basilica. On the left is the Temple of Athena Polias, which belongs to the Acropolis of ancient Ialyssos.

Left page. Top: A panoramic view of the Gulf of Ialyssos from Mt. Phileremos. Bottom: Tourist installations along the Bay of Ialyssos.

Haghios Georgios Chostos, a subterranean chapel with frescoes painted in the eclectic style of the era of the Knights. On the long walls of the chapel's nave is a procession of kneeling Knights and their patron saints. They are facing Christ and the Apostles Peter and Paul who are painted on the east wall. On the vault are depicted scenes from the life of the Virgin Mary and from the Passion of Christ. A westbound monumental road started from approximately the center of the plateau. It was interspersed with scenes from the Passion of Christ, in the manner of the Calvary of Western pilgrimage sites.
The Byzantine fortress was at the eastern end of the plateau. It was used by the Byzantines of Johannes Kantakouzenos during the Genoese siege of 1248. It served as the headquarters of the Knights and of Suleiman the Magnificent in 1306 and 1522 respectively.

The reconstructed Monastery of the era of the Knights on Mt. Phileremos. Top: A shady stoa. Bottom: The courtyard of the Monastery.

Right page: Views of the Temple of Athena Polias. Third century B.C.

IALYSSOS

The site is known from Minoan and Mycenean times. The settlements were scattered in the surrounding hills; at the top of Mt. Phileremos was the Acropolis of Ancient Ialyssos, which was called Achaia in remembrance of the origins of the Mycenean settlers. The remains of the doric Temple of Athena Polias date from the 3rd or 2nd century B.C. but the local cult of the goddess was six or seven centuries older. The temple was destroyed in the 5th or 6th century A.D. and the cult of the central female deity of the ancient world was succeeded by the worship of the Virgin Mary. On the south slope of Mt. Phileremos, near the top, is a reconstructed 4th century B.C. monumental doric fountain.

The Early Christian baptistery and the Abbot's House of the reconstructed Monastery of the Knights. Bottom: Haghios Georghios Chostos. West entrance and view of interior.

Right Page. Haghios Georghios Chostos. Top: Fresco showing a kneeling Knight. Bottom: View of frescoes on the vault.

THE VALLEY OF THE BUTTERFLIES

On the way to the archaeological site of Kamiros, 25 kilometers from the city of Rhodes, is the Valley of the Butterflies, an area of outstanding natural beauty, near the villages of Kremasti and Paradeissi. It is a protected tourist site, landscaped for hiking, with streams, ponds, wooden bridges and shady footpaths. The butterflies are of the species *Euplagia quadripunctaria* and they live in the cool valley from May until September. They are attracted to the area by the fragrant resin of the bark of the semi-indigenous *Liquidambar orientalis*, which is a tall tree, indigenous in Asia Minor, resembling a plane tree.

Right: Drawing of a butterfly with open and closed wings.
Bottom: Butterflies on the foliage of the Liquidambar orientalis.

Left page: Bridges and ponds in the Valley of the Butterflies.

THE MONASTERY OF THE VIRGIN MARY AT KALOPETRA

The Monastery of Kalopetra, which overlooks the valley of the Butterflies, is dedicated to the Dormition of the Virgin Mary. It was built on the ruins of an earlier monastery by Alexander Ypselantes, the Greek ruler of Walachia, Rumania following his rescue from rough seas in the nearby area of Phanoi. Ypselantes had fallen into the Sultan's disfavor and was exiled in Rhodes for a few years.
The beaches near Kalopetra are picturesque and hospitable. The remains of a doric temple dedicated to the patron of agriculture Apollo Erethimios, a small theater (5th-4th century B.C.) and the lovely tourist village of Theologos are on the way to the city of Rhodes, not far from Kalopetra.

Top: Interior view of the monastic church showing the cobbled floor. Bottom: The choir screen of the church.

Left page. Top: The monastic church dedicated to the Dormition of the Virgin. The facade bears a plaque with the donor's name, Alexandros Ypselantes, and the date 1782-84. Bottom: A panoramic view from Kalopetra near the Valley of the Butterflies.

Next pages: The beach near Kalopetra. Seascape and a fisherman mending nets.

KAMIROS

Built on an amphitheater-like slope in a fertile area, Kamiros was one of the three major cities of archaic Rhodes. From the 6th century B.C., Kamiros had its own coin; on one face it bore a fig leaf, reflecting the agrarian nature of the local economy. Ialyssos and Lindos, the other two major archaic city-states, minted coins a century later. Although they assumed secondary importance, all three cities continued to prosper after the foundation of the city of Rhodes.
The wealth of Kamiros is apparent in its scattered architectural remains, which extend to coast, and in the finds from the surrounding hills, now on display at the Archaeological Museum of Rhodes. Among the Museum exhibits are the vases from Phikelloura, a site to the west of the residential area. An important category in Late Orientalizing Ancient Greek pottery has been named after Phikelloura, where the Rhodian ware was found. In the pottery of this type, groups of motifs are arranged in parallel

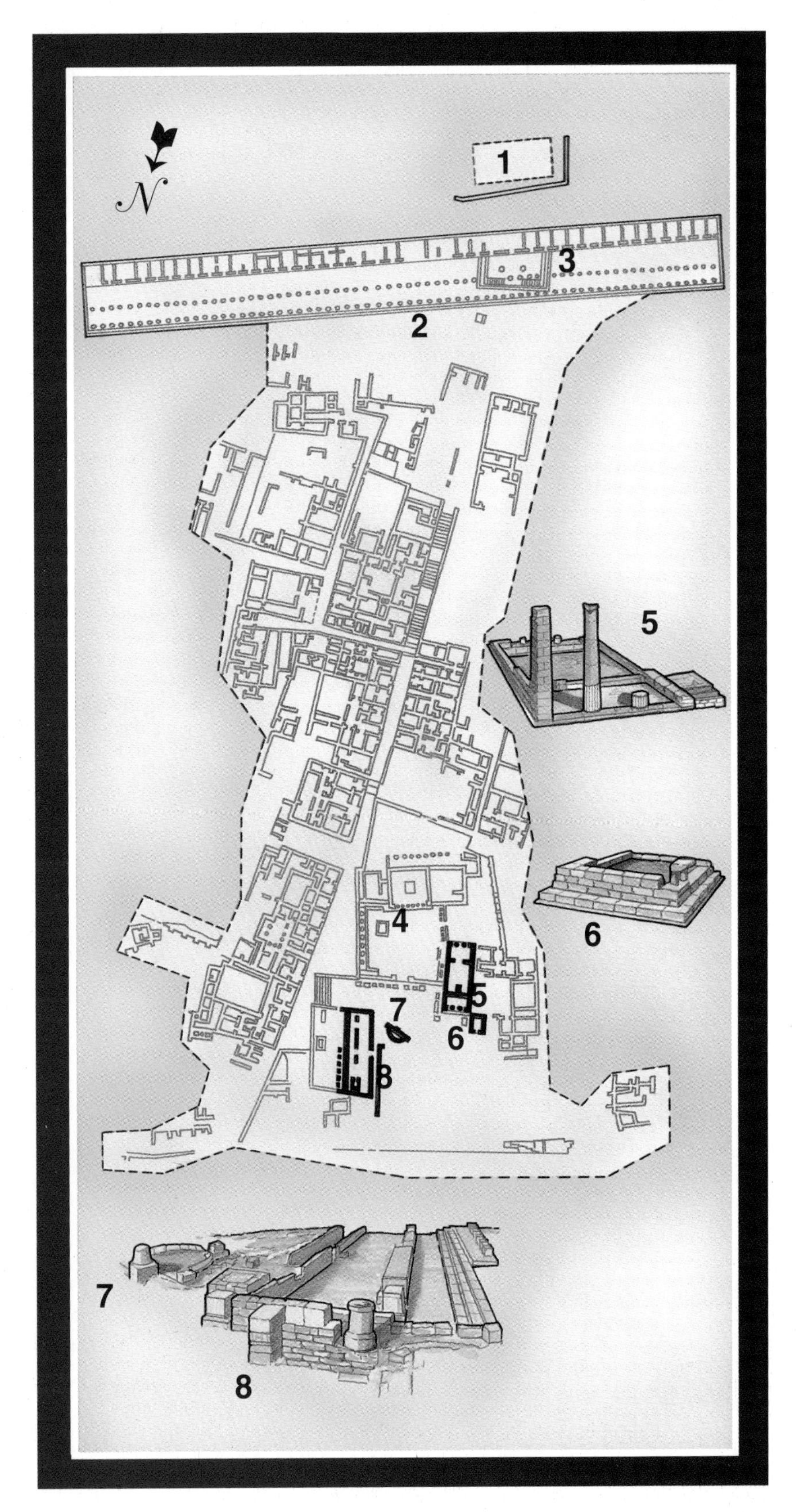

Kamiros. Plan of the excavated part of the residential area and drawings of the remains of the Hellenistic temple in antis, of its treasury, of the semicircular exedra and of an enclosed space for offerings.

LEGEND

1 Temple of Athena Polias	4 Fountain	6 Treasure
2 Stoa	5 Hellenistic temple in antis	7 Exedra
3 Cistern		8 Area for votive offerings

Next page. Top: View of the residential area from the Acropolis. In the distance below is the sector with the sacred buildings. Bottom: View of the ancient town from the northwest.

The Hellenistic temple at the lowest sector of the excavations.

Next page. Top: View of the buildings to the southeast of the Hellenistic temple. Bottom: The square of the monumental fountain.

bands in a way that enhances the shape of the vase. Various patterns and animal and bird figures mainly are rendered in a lively way. There is regularity in the repetition of motifs, though no mechanical accuracy.
Kamiros was the homeland of archaic epic poet Peisander, who was considered to rank after Homer and Hesiod. In his "Heraclea", he recounted the life and labors of Hercules, the mythological ancestor of the Rhodians.
Kamiros has been connected by myth to Althaimenes, son of Katreus, the King of Crete, and grandson of Minos. Althaimenes left Crete and settled in Kamiros because an oracle had predicted that Katreus would be killed by one of his children. Years later, the king of Crete arrived in Rhodes to find his son. The prophesy came true, as Althaimenes took his father for a pirate and killed him. When he realized what he had done, he prayed to be swallowed up by the Earth. The reference to the Earth in the myth ties in with the local worship of the Gods of the Mills, which also dates from prehistoric times. Zeus Mylantios (Zeus of the Mills) and the Nymph Himalia taught people how to grind grain and make bread.
Three urban sectors can be distinguished in the excavated part of the residential area. At the lowest point on the slope is an important religious center built around a square on two levels. Here was a Hellenistic temple in antis, its treasury, a small ionic temple, a monumental fountain, a semicircular exedra and many offerings, among which were those of the family of the philosopher Panaetius. A broad stair between the two levels of the square leads to a

street which traverses the housing district and reaches the highest and southernmost point of the excavated site, the Acropolis of Kamiros. On the Acropolis are the great Hellenistic doric stoa, the archaic cistern and the Temple of Athena Polias, which dates from the late third or early second century B.C.

Life in the area was uninterrupted from the prehistoric era to the Early Christian times. Additions to the buildings dating from various periods of history can be observed in the ruins of the city. Kamiros acquired a wall during the Hellenistic period and a regular city plan after the earthquakes of 226 B.C.

In Kamiros stand out the remains of monumental structures, of public baths and of a house with a peristyle court. There is a very good drainage system and a remarkable layout of street and urban space. The Hippodameian system of city planning has been adapted to an irregular, sloping terrain.

Views of the housing district.

Right page. Top: The archaic cistern on the Acropolis of Kamiros. Bottom: Looking north from the Acropolis.

THE FORTRESS OF CRETENIA

Situated near the villages of Kamiros Skala and Cretenia, almost halfway along the northwest coast, the Fortress of Cretenia was rebuilt in 1472 during the rule of Grand Master Giovanni Battista degli Orsini. Additions were made during the rule of Pierre d'Aubusson and Fabrizio del Carretto. In the fortress is a church dedicated to St. George, dating from the era of the Knights.

Top: General view of the Fortress. Bottom and right page: The view toward the coast with the islets of Alimnia, Tragoussa, Strogyli and Makri in the distance.

THE FORTRESS OF MONOLITHOS

The Byzantine fortress at Monolithos was repaired in 1476 during the rule af Grand Master Pierre d'Aubusson. It controlled the south part of the west coast of the island. Inside the fortress are the aisleless church of St. Pantaleon, the remains of another church, ruins of houses and cisterns.

CRETENIA

One of the loveliest traditional villages in Rhodes, Cretenia, is situated approximately five kilometers south of the coastal village of Kamiros Skala. The villagers of Cretenia are Cretans by origin and they are farmers and livestock breeders.

Views of the Fortress.

Next page. Cretenia. A view of the village, of the Museum of Popular Art, local costumes and a loom in the Museum.

MOUNT ATABYROS

According to myth, the Sanctuary of Zeus Atabyrios, on top of the highest mountain in Rhodes, was founded by Althaimenes, who had come to Kamiros from Crete. In Byzantine times, a church dedicated to Haghios Johannes was built here. The Monastery of Artamitis was founded in the 9th or 10th century at the east foot of the mountain; it was also a great intellectual center during the rule of the Knights. Greeks and Westerners used to study in the Monastery's library and monks copied rare manuscripts. The Monastery was destroyed and rebuilt during the Turkish occupation. Today only the church survives and is dedicated to St. John the Theologian.

Cultivated land on the fertile slopes, a wooded slope and a villager on Mt. Atabyros.

Top: The village of Embonas on the slope of Mt. Atabyros. Bottom: Local handwoven goods in the village shops.

Right page. Traditional costumes and dances in Embonas.

EMBONAS

Built at an altitude of 850 meters on the northwest slope of Mt. Atabyros, Embonas is the highest village in Rhodes. It has approximately 1,500 inhabitants of Cretan descent. In about two hours, with a local guide, one can walk from Embonas to the top of Mt .Atabyros, where one can enjoy a panoramic view of the entire island.
The village is known for its healthy climate and its good wine. The local economy is based on the cultivation of vines and olive trees. Embonas is also famous for the handwoven textiles and other handicrafts which are produced locally. Some of the villagers still wear their ocal costumes. Traditional

The Church of the Virgin Mary in Embonas. Top: The interior. Bottom: Detail of the choir screen.

Left page. Top left: Entrance and bell tower.Top right: The pulpit. Bottom: West facade.

feasts and dances featuring local bands and folk dance groups often take place in the summer. The village houses preserve the Rhodian architecture and decoration. The main village church is dedicated to the Dormition of the Virgin Mary, which is celebrated on 15 August. The west facade of the church is plain, with a neoclassical door frame. In the interior there are lovely icons and frescoes and a carved wooden pulpit and choir screen.

Frescoes in the interior of Haghios Nikolaos.

Right page. Southwest view of the church.

HAGHIOS NIKOLAOS AT PHOUNDOUKLI

Near the village of Dimylia, in a mountainous area on the slopes of Mt. Prophet Elias, the quatrefoil church of Haghios Nikolaos is surrounded by vegetation. It contains 14th-15th century frescoes. On the west conch is depicted the family of the donors. Deisis (Prayer) is in the choir apse and Christ Pantocrator (Christ All-Ruling) in the dome. Very few remains survive of the monastery that existed at Haghios Nikolaos until the 19th century.

Top: Mt. Prophet Elias. Chapel dedicated to the Saint.
Bottom: A forest road on Mt. Prophet Elias.

Right page. The new monastic church of Haghios Nektarios. The bishop's throne and a view of the church interior with frescoes executed in the Byzantine manner.

MOUNT PROPHET ELIAS

The Monastery of Prophet Elias on top of the mountain is visited by many pilgrims on 20 July every year, the date when the Saint is celebrated by the Church. On the wooded mountain slopes, visitors can tour the lovely village of Salakos and see the mountain cottages and a hotel that were built during the Italian occupation in the style of Alpine architecture.

HAGHIOS NEKTARIOS

In an idyllic site near Archipolis is a new monastery dedicated to the miraculous saint Nektarios.

THE SOUTHEAST COAST

Along the southeast coast, there are lovely villages, arable plains and organized beaches with large hotel complexes and many furnished apartments. The largest bays are those of Kallithea, Aphandou, Vlycha, and Lardos.

Not far from the city of Rhodes is the lovely traditional village of Koskinou, situated approximately four kilometers from the beach. The houses in the village preserve the Rhodian architecture, with cobbled courtyards and traditional interiors decorated with colorful ceramics and textiles. Fruit trees mainly are grown in the area. The village of Aphandou was built on a site invisible from the sea, so as to be protected from the raids of the Saracen pirates. The Church of Panayia Katholiki was erected on the site of an Early Christian basilica. It is adorned with frescoes from the era of the Knights. At the nearby village of Kolymbia are the remains of an Early Christian basilica with an elaborate mosaic floor. To the southwest of Mt. Tsambika is Archangelos, a large picturesque village with a medieval fortress, pottery workshops, a local carpet industry and a beautiful beach within easy reach. Near the charming village of Malona, to the north of the Fortress of Pheraklos, is Haghia Agathe, a 12th century church with fresco paintings, built in the hollow of a rock.

At the northernmost tip of the island, on a site called Vroulia, are the remains of a small archaic fortified town with a rectangular grid plan, dating from around 700 B.C.

Bottom and next page: Beaches at Kallithea.

PHALIRAKI

Situated at the south end of the Bay of Kallithea, Phaliraki is undergoing a period of rapid tourist development. Large hotel complexes and apartments for rent guarantee carefree holidays. The beaches are well organized and adequately equipped for marine sports. At the north end of the bay, the disused Thermal Baths of Kallithea are architecturally interesting. They were built in the early 20th century to utilize the mineral springs. Even though the spa is no longer in use, one can swim in the crystal clear waters of the sea near the rocks, at the sandy beach, or at the little harbor lined with palm trees.

Beaches and sea views in Phaliraki.

Next pages: A panoramic view, beaches and coves in the tourist area of the Bay of Kallithea.

SEVEN SPRINGS

Near the village of Kolymbia, Seven Springs is a beautifully landscaped natural park with little wooden bridges, small waterfalls, and two ponds connected by a big tunnel. Tall plane trees and pines shade the cool footpaths of this idyllic site.

THE MONASTERY OF TSAMBIKA

On top of Mt. Tsambika was the Byzantine Monastery of Panayia, from which only the cells and the aisleless church survive. Childless women used to come and pray here in order to conceive. The new Monastery, which is also dedicated to Panayia, is found to the southwest of the old one, a little lower down the slope of the mountain. The ascent of Mt. Tsambika is recommended both as good exercise and for the panoramic view it offers.

Top: A view of Seven Springs.
Bottom: Mount Tsambika and the nearby beach.

Left page: A natural spring, a little bridge, and a small dam in Seven Springs.

Top: The Knights of the Order of St. John of Jerusalem first seized Pheraklos when Rhodes was ceded to them by the Genoese Vignolo da Vignola. The Fortress was rebuilt in 1470 by Grand Master Giovanni Battista degli Orsini. It commands the coast from Lindos in the south to Phaliraki in the north. At the foot of the Fortress is the resort village of Charaki. Left: Steep rocks below the Fortress. Here above: a fishermen's house.

Preceding pages : Panoramic views of the coast to the north and south of Mt. Tsambika. Views of the west entrance and of the choir screen of the church.

LINDOS

The Acropolis of Lindos from the east.

The traditional village of Lindos sprawls along the west foot of the cliff of the Acropolis. In the village, there are white, cube-shaped buildings as well as square porous buildings with isodomic masonry and Byzantine, Islamic and medieval West European relief ornament on the facade. The stately homes of Lindos were erected during the era of economic prosperity of the town, in the 17th and 18th centuries, when Lindian ships resumed activity in the Dodecanese. Lindian homes maintain the plan of the Hellenistic house, which develops around a central courtyard and is protected from noise and passers-by by a high wall. The reception room on the ground floor and the courtyards are paved with pebbles from the sea which form the shapes of boats, and geometric and plant motifs. The reception room on the first floor and the ground floor rooms are decorated with paintings on the wooden ceiling. They contain hand-carved wooden furniture, the famous local embroidery and lacework and, the so-called Lindian, multicolored ceramics.

Near the northwest entrance to the village is the spacious Church of Panayia. A former monastic church it has a free-cross plan with a dome on an octagonal drum. There are geometric patterns on the cobbled floor of the church. The bishop's throne and the 17th century choir screen are hand-carved in wood. The church contains frescoes by the painter Grego-

Top: The Acropolis and the village of Lindos.

Right: Aegean architecture. Two house entrances with a Neoclassical and a Renaissance door frame respectively. Paved and cobbled streets in the village.

Left and top: Lindian handicrafts. Bottom: Ascent to the Acropolis by donkey.

Next page. Reconstruction of the Acropoli of Lindos.

rios of Symi dating from 1779. At the foot of the Acropolis, Haghios Georghios Chostos is a Byzantine aisleless church with an inscribed cross plan. It contains frescoes dating from the 8th or 9th century, from the 12th and from the 18th century.
An ancient theater and a big orthogonal court which is surrounded by a doric stoa have been excavated at the southwest foot of the Acropolis, near the church of Haghios Stephanos. Two important inscriptions were found in the same area. One contains the Register of the Priests of Athena Lindia from 406 B.C. until A.D. 47 and the other, the Chronicle of the Temple of Lindos, dating from 99 B.C. The Chronicle was written by Timachidas of Lindos. It mentions three miraculous deeds of the Goddess Athena and lists the most important offerings to the Temple starting from those mentioned in mythology. The two inscriptions and other finds from Lindos are in the National Museum in Copenhagen. They were taken there in the early 20th century by the Danish archaeologists who excavated Lindos.
Ancient Lindos extended inland and toward the west. It occupied an area larger than the present-day village. According to the myth, it took its name from Lindos, the grandson of Helios and Rode. Lindos was the brother of Ialyssos and Kamiros, who were the eponymous heroes of the other two important archaic cities on the island. Another myth interprets the naming of the three cities in a different way. Lindos, Ialyssos and Kamiros took their names from the three daughters of Danaos, who was the founder of the Temple of Athena Lindia. The Telchinae, the mythical creatures who sculpted the first likenesses of the gods, have also been connected with the foundation of Lindos.
Architectural monuments from various periods in the history of the site up to medieval times are to be found on the Acropolis of Lindos. The Boucopeion, a small sanctuary for sacrifices, is on the north face of the rock. It was founded there during the Dorian invasion because, in the old ritual, animal sacrifice was prohibited in the Acropolis. At a small plateau toward the entrance to the Acropolis, there are a round exedra and the stern of a ship dating from 180 B.C., carved in the rock. On the ship was a bronze statue of the sea hero Agesander by the sculptor Pythocritos. An altar or a pedestal for a statue stands in front of the exedra. In an epigram inscribed on the left end of the exedra in the 3rd or 4rth century A.D., a priest of Athena called Aglochartos mentions that he planted olive trees in the Sacred Wood on the Acropolis.
To the left of the entrance to the Acropolis is the north facade of the Palace of the Commander of the Knights. Grand Master Foulques de Villaret sought refuge in Lindos when the Knights staged a rebellion against him. He was finally obliged by the Pope to return to Avignon. Next to the Commandery are the ruins of the three-aisled Byzantine church of Haghios Johannes, dating from the 13th century. The big Hellenistic stoa spreads out in the center of the Acropolis. In antiquity, it formed a monumental unit on the same axis with the Propylaea, which were similar to the ones on the Acropolis of Athens, and with the Temple of Athena Lindia, on the highest spot, at the edge of the cliff.

The worship of Athena initially took place outdoors, in the Sacred Wood of the Goddess, on the Acropolis. Her cult image was a wooden likeness. In the Geometric period, a temple was built and the first statue of the Goddess was made. The tyrant of Lindos, Cleobulus, one of the Seven Sages of ancient Greece, built a new temple in the middle of the 6th century B.C. This temple was destroyed by fire and was rebuilt in the second half of the 4th century B.C. A greater statue of the Goddess was dedicated to the Temple at that time. The body was made of wood covered with gold and the limbs were made of marble or gold and ivory.

A monumental staircase connected the Hellenistic stoa with the Propylaea. Another smaller staircase joined the level of the stoa with the northeast part of the Acropolis, where a small Roman temple was built in the 3rd century A.D. Many offerings were to be seen all around the Acropolis. Among them was a painting of Hercules by Parrhasius of Ephesus. The Sacred Wood probably protected visitors from the sun and the winds before the completion of the covered spaces of the stoa and the Propylaea during the Hellenistic period.

Top: Stairway leading to the Acropolis entrance. On the left, above the steps, is the Palace of the Commander of the Knights. Bottom: Round exedra and stern of a ship carved in the rock, at the bottom of the steps.

Right page: The steep rock at the southern tip of the Acropolis. The reconstruction is being carried out at the east wing of the Hellenistic stoa.

Top: From the Acropolis entrance, the ascent toward the Hellenistic stoa and the Propylaea. On the extreme right, part of the Byzantine fortifications can be seen on the base of the wall. Bottom: The east wing of the stoa.

Right page. Top: Looking from the Temenos of Athena Lindia toward the east wing of the stoa. In the foreground are marble pedestals for the offerings to the temple. Bottom: A view of the east wing of the stoa and of the coast toward the east.

Top: Preservation works on columns of the east wing of the stoa. Bottom: Marble pedestals for offerings, the walls, and the view from the Acropolis toward the north and the east.

Left page. Top: The east wing of the stoa and the retaining wall of the Propylaea in the center. Bottom: The Church of Haghios Johannes.

Left page and top: The Harbor of St. Paul. It is said that St. Paul visited Lindos on his way to Rome.
Bottom: Panoramic views, little harbors and beaches near Lindos.

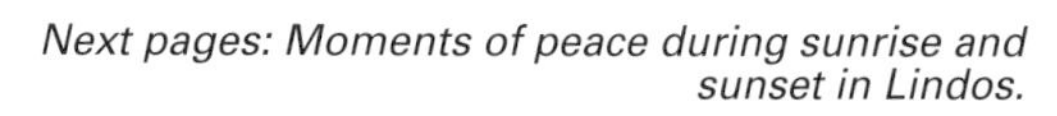

Next pages: Moments of peace during sunrise and sunset in Lindos.

Popular beaches in Lardos.

THE BAY OF LARDOS

Ancient Lartos was to the southeast of Lindos. The area is known for its grey marble, which was used in ancient buildings and sculptural monuments. Surrounded by vineyards, the present-day village of Lardos is built according to traditional architecture. The Bay of Lardos has recently undergone great tourist development. It has luxurious hotel and furnished apartment complexes. However, it is still possible to enjoy a quiet vacation here. A short distance inland are the farming villages of Mesanagros and Kattavia. A hike to the solitary peninsula of Prassonissi is recommended. It lies at the southermost tip of Rhodes and has beautiful sand dunes. Prassonissi is connected with the mainland in the summer only as the level of the sea rises in the winter.

THE NUNNERY OF PANAYIA IPSENI

The Nunnery of Panayia Ipseni is found in an idyllic location near the village of Lardos. The area is a nature lover's delight. The Nunnery was founded in 1855 by the monk-priest Meletios.
It has lovely frescoes and a choir screen carved in wood. In addition to the silver icon of Panayia Ipseni, there is a painted icon of the Virgin Mary by Pothetos Zoides from Chania, Crete, dating from 1856.

Top: The Nunnery of Panayia Ipseni.
Bottom: The church of the Monastery of the Archangel Michael at Thari.

Top: A view of the interior of the monastic church with the carved, wooden choir screen. Bottom: Frescoes on the vault of the church. The Resurrection and the Transfiguration of Christ.

THE MONASTERY OF THE ARCHANGEL MICHAEL AT THARI

The Monastery of the Archangel Michael at Thari is situated on a mountain slope south of the village of Laerma, approximately west of Lindos. The monastic church was built in a free-cross plan on the remains of an Early Christian church. The oldest part of the church is the apse; it was constructed in the 12th or the 13th century. The dome dates from two centuries later. The west part of the church was built around 1600. The hand-carved wooden choir screen dates from the 18th century. The Christ Pantocrator is depicted on the dome and on the apse is the Deisis and the Prophets Isaiah and Ezekiel.

CONTENTS

Introduction . . . . .page 3

RHODES - THE CITY OF THE KNIGHTS . . . . " 7

The Acropolis of Rhodes . . . . " 62
The Archaeological Museum . . . . " 28
The City within the Walls . . . . " 39
History of the City of the Knights . . . . " 7
The Museum of Popular Art . . . . " 38
The New Town near the Port . . . . " 54
The Old Town and the Walls . . . . " 48
The Palace of the Grand Master . . . . " 20
The Street of the Knights . . . . " 16
A Visit to the City of the Knights . . . . " 11

THE NORTHWEST COAST . . . . " 65

Cretenia . . . . " 86
Embonas . . . . " 90
The Fortress of Cretenia . . . . " 84
The Fortress of Monolithos . . . . " 86
Haghios Nektarios . . . . " 96
Haghios Nikolaos at Phoundoukli page94
Ialyssos . . . . " 70
Kamiros . . . . " 78
The Monastery of the Virgin Mary at Kalopetra . . . . " 75
Mount Atabyros . . . . " 89
Mount Prophet Elias . . . . " 96
Phileremos . . . . " 67
The Valley of the Butterflies . . . . " 73

THE SOUTHEAST COAST . . . . " 98

The Bay of Lardos . . . . " 125
The Fortress of Pheraklos . . . . " 108
Phaliraki . . . . " 101
Seven Springs . . . . " 105

LINDOS . . . . " 109

The Monastery of the Archangel Michael at Thari . . . . " 127
The Monastery of Tsambika . . . . " 105
The Nunnery of Panayia Ipseni . . . . " 126

ISBN 88-8029-465-2

* * *

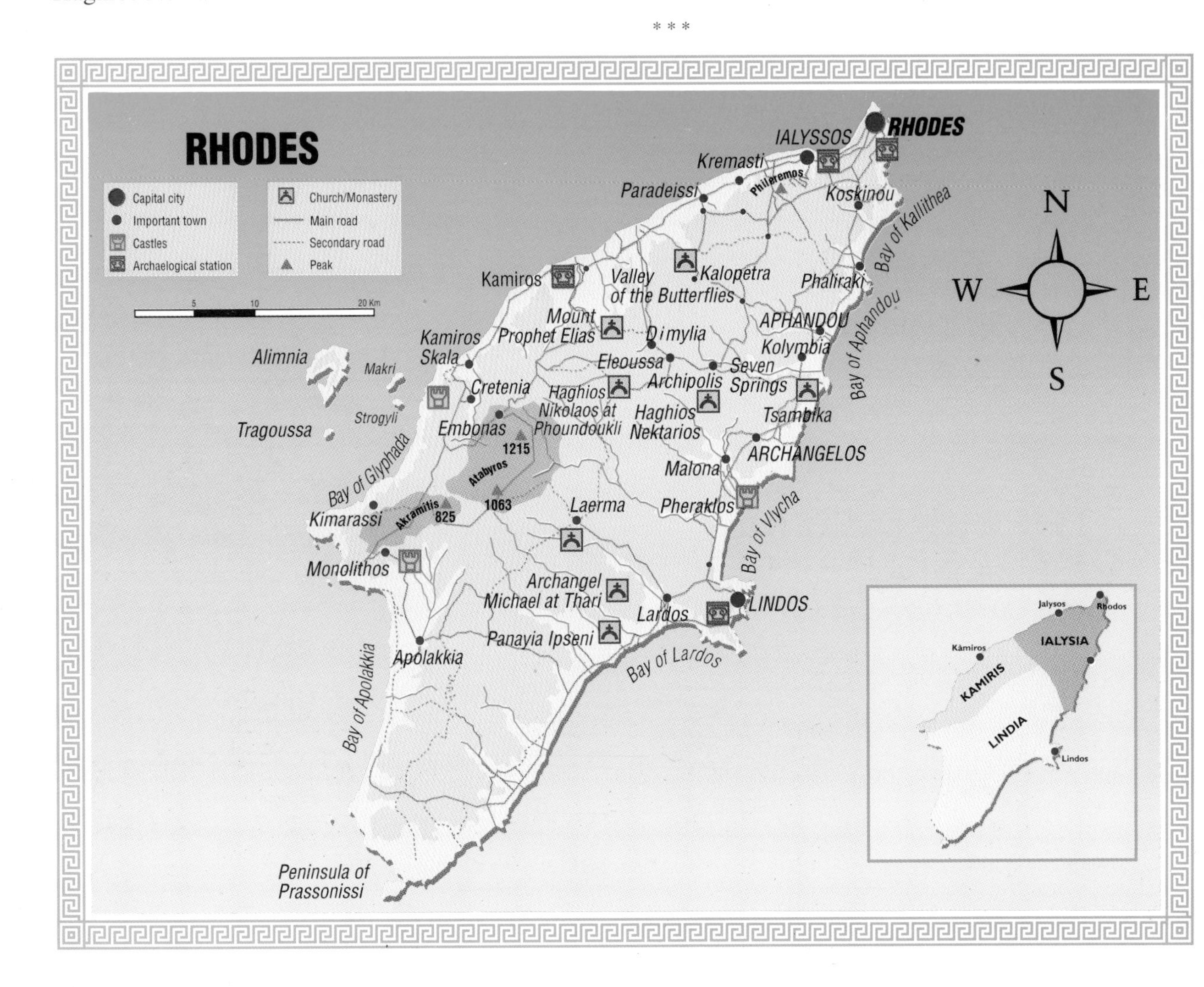